INCREDIBLES 2

The Science of
Super Powers

An Incredibles Discovery Book

By Kris Hirschmann

Illustrated by the Disney Storybook Art Team

Special thanks to Professor Suveen N. Mathaudhu,
University of California, Riverside

Lerner Publications ◆ Minneapolis

Foreword

To me, *The Incredibles* has always been about nostalgia. When the movie splashed across the silver screen in 2004, it flashed me back to a time and place where comic books could be bought for a few cents, and spies and their clever gadgets were everywhere in entertainment and the daily news. These were times of unprecedented advancements in science and technology.

When I was a kid, heroes with super powers, super-gadgets, and super-vehicles were what really ignited my imagination. Alongside the many new technologies emerging, it was this imaginary world that inspired me and many of my peers to become scientists and engineers.

When you read this book as a family, it is our hope that revisiting the timeless, exciting world of *The Incredibles* will inspire the next generation of science, technology, engineering, arts, and math (STEAM) "Supers-in-Training" who will be eager to understand our universe, shape a better world for the future, and take down a few villains along the way.

Suveen N. Mathaudhu, PhD
University of California, Riverside

Lerner Publications Company
A division of Lerner Publishing Group, Inc.
241 First Avenue North
Minneapolis, MN 55401 USA

For reading levels and more information, look up this title at www.lernerbooks.com.

Main body text set in Mikado Regular 12/20.
Typeface provided by HVD Fonts.

Library of Congress Cataloging-in-Publication Data

Names: Hirschmann, Kris, 1967- author. | Disney Storybook
    Artists, illustrator.
Title: The science of super powers : an Incredibles discovery book / by
    Kris Hirschmann ; illustrated by the Disney Storybook Artists.
Description: Minneapolis : Lerner Publications, [2020] | Series: Disney
    learning discovery books | Audience: Age 7–11. | Audience: Grade 4 to 6. |
    Includes index.
Identifiers: LCCN 2018049359 (print) | LCCN 2018056621 (ebook) | ISBN
    9781541561434 (eb pdf) | ISBN 9781541554894 (lb : alk. paper) | ISBN
    9781541573901 (pb : alk. paper)
Subjects: LCSH: Science—Miscellanea—Juvenile literature. | Human body—Juvenile
    literature. | Incredibles (Motion picture)—Juvenile literature.
Classification: LCC Q175.2 (ebook) | LCC Q175.2 .H57 2020 (print) | DDC 500—dc23

LC record available at https://lccn.loc.gov/2018049359

Manufactured in the United States of America
1-45807-42689-12/26/2018

CONTENTS

MEET THE INCREDIBLES!

The Incredibles are a family of Supers. This means they are people with superhuman powers. When Supers use their powers, they are careful to protect their identities with masks and Supersuits. To most people, the Incredibles are just plain old Bob and Helen Parr and their three children—Violet, Dash, and Jack-Jack.

Mr. Incredible/
Bob Parr

Elastigirl/
Helen Parr

Jack-Jack
Parr

Violet Parr

Dash Parr

In the second *Incredibles* film, a villain named the Screenslaver threatens all Supers. The family has to summon all their powers and work together. What exactly are their super powers? How do they work? Will the Incredibles defeat the Screenslaver? And what amazing science will they harness along the way? Read on to discover the real science of the Supers!

SUPER STRENGTH

Not only does Mr. Incredible have superhuman strength, but so do some people, animals, and insects! Let's look at some real-world examples.

Superhuman Feats

Real people sometimes have bursts of super strength during emergencies. There are many cases of people lifting cars off accident victims. Scientists think that under stress, our bodies can be flooded with a strength-boosting **hormone** called adrenaline.

Beetle Mania

Scientists have dubbed the dung beetle the world's strongest creature. These insects can pull over 1,000 times their own weight. That's like a person pulling six fully loaded double-decker buses!

Dung beetle

Animal Athletes and Power Lifters

 A dung beetle can pull more than 1,000 times its body weight.

 A human, Eddie Hall, can lift close to three times his body weight—but only for a very short time.

 A leafcutter ant can lift fifty times its body weight.

 A tiger can carry two times its body weight over a long distance.

 A gorilla can lift ten times its body weight.

 An elephant can carry more than one and a half times its body weight.

Prostheses

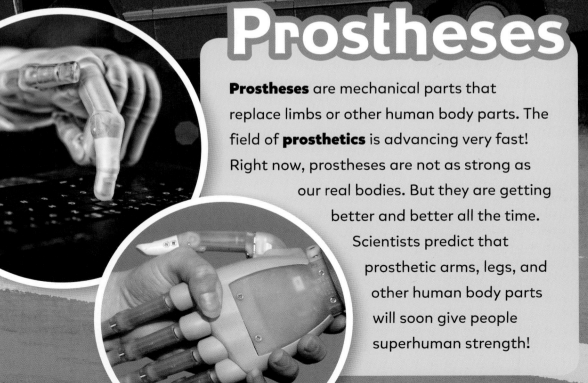

Prostheses are mechanical parts that replace limbs or other human body parts. The field of **prosthetics** is advancing very fast! Right now, prostheses are not as strong as our real bodies. But they are getting better and better all the time. Scientists predict that prosthetic arms, legs, and other human body parts will soon give people superhuman strength!

GETTING STRONGER

Just because Mr. Incredible has super strength doesn't mean he can go without **exercise**. How do our **muscles** work, and how does exercise change them? Let's find out!

Muscle Types

Your body has three different types of muscles. Two types, the **smooth** muscles (muscles found in your organs) and the **cardiac** muscle (your heart), work automatically. That means you can't control them. You *can* control the third type— the **skeletal** muscles. There are about 650 skeletal muscles in your body. These are the muscles that make you move.

Types of Muscles

Cardiac **Skeletal** **Smooth**

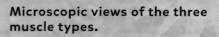

Microscopic views of the three muscle types.

The Frame

The skeletal muscles are attached to your bones. The bones work like a frame. They give the muscles something hard to pull against. Without bones, you would just be a wiggling blob!

Skeletal muscles attach to bone.

Muscle Growth

Exercise tears your muscles a little bit. Afterward, your body adds new muscle **fibers** to fix the rips. These fibers make your muscles a little bit bigger and stronger. The more you exercise, the more this happens, and the stronger you get!

BENDY BODIES

Elastigirl is extremely **flexible**. Real people could never bend quite that much! But some people and animals are bendier than others. Let's check out a few interesting examples.

Babies

When human babies are born, their skeletons are not fully formed. Some parts are made of rubbery stuff called **cartilage** instead of bone. Much of this cartilage is found in the joints. This makes babies very bendy. As babies grow, the cartilage turns into bone, so they get less flexible.

Sharks

A shark doesn't have any bones at all. Its whole skeleton is made of cartilage! This makes sharks very flexible. They can twist themselves quickly to catch speedy prey.

Contortion

People called **contortionists** train their bodies to bend in unusual ways. They usually start training when they are very young. They do hours of stretching every day to keep their muscles and joints loose.

PARACHUTES

What do you do if you are falling from the sky? If you're Elastigirl, you stretch your body into a parachute and float safely to the ground! Real human bodies don't work this way, but people can use **technology** to get the same effect. And some animals *do* have built-in parachutes. Let's see these things at work.

How Parachutes Work

A **force** called **gravity** pulls a falling person downward. A parachute's fabric spreads out and pushes against the air. This force is called **air resistance**. The air resistance works against gravity and slows the person to a safe speed.

Flying Squirrels

Flying squirrels have flaps of skin that stretch from their front paws to hind feet. A flying squirrel can jump from a tall tree, then spread its legs wide. The skin flaps open and create air resistance. This force slows the squirrel down. It glides instead of falling.

Wingsuits

People can wear **wingsuits** that let them glide just like flying squirrels! Wingsuits have flaps of parachute fabric between the arms and legs. Wearing the suit, a person leaps off a cliff or out of a plane. The person spreads their arms and legs in an X position. The wingsuit creates air resistance and lets the person soar.

13

INVISIBILITY

Now you see her, now you don't! Violet has the power to turn **invisible** whenever she wants to. Lucky her! True invisibility is not possible for people or animals. But with a little help from nature, science, and technology, we can come close. Let's take a look—or try to, anyway!

Invisibility Cloaks

Scientists are trying to create invisibility cloaks for people to wear. These cloaks, made of something called **metamaterial**, would work by bending light rays. So far, scientists have only been able to make very small objects invisible. People are way too big. But scientists are still trying!

Camouflage

Camouflage is the ability to blend in with one's surroundings. Some animals are camouflage experts! The caterpillar in this picture looks exactly like a twig. Can you see it? If you didn't know it was there, you might never notice it. Other animals camouflage themselves with color or skin **texture**.

Stealth Planes

Stealth planes are built to be nearly invisible to **radar**. Radar is a system that uses energy waves to detect objects. Machines send these waves out. When they hit a regular plane, they bounce back. The machine gets the echoes and "sees" the object. Stealth planes have special shapes, colors, and paints that scatter most of the waves instead of echoing them back. So, according to radar, the plane is about the size of a bumblebee. The next generation of stealth planes will look even smaller on radar—more like mosquitoes! Tricky!

FORCE FIELDS

When trouble approaches, WHAM! Violet throws up a **force field**. It blocks anything that might hurt her or her family. Real force fields exist in nature. Just like Violet's invisible **barrier**, they stop certain things from getting through.

Earth's Armor

Our planet has its very own force field! Earth is surrounded by an invisible **magnetic** field. This field blocks many **particles** streaming from the sun. The particles flow right around Earth and into space. That's lucky for us, because these particles would hurt living plants and animals—including people!

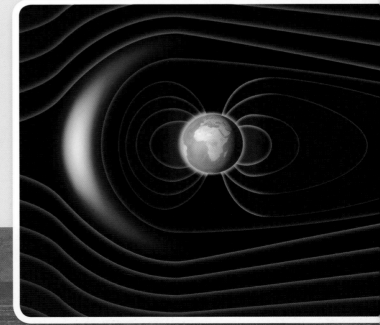

Magnetic Poles

Magnets have two poles. Scientists call them north and south. *Opposite* poles (north and south) **attract** each other. *Like* poles (north and north, or south and south) push against or **repel** each other. This push is very strong. Try to shove two like poles together, and you'll see for yourself. An invisible force field makes it impossible!

Static Field

Static **electricity** can form an invisible field that makes your hair stand on end. Rub a balloon against your hair to see and feel it for yourself! This type of electricity can also zap you, like when you touch a doorknob after walking across a carpeted surface. A spark snaps against your finger as the electricity discharges. OW!

SUPER SPEED

ZOOM! What was that? It was Dash, zipping past at superhuman speed! Dash can run close to 200 miles (321.9 km) per hour. What would happen if a real human ran that fast? And just how fast *are* people and animals, anyway? Let's find out!

Friction

When people move, their bodies rub against lots of things, such as their clothing, the ground, the air, and even themselves. Rubbing creates a force called **friction**, and friction makes heat. Rub your palms together quickly, and you'll see. HOT! Dash wears a friction-resistant suit so his clothes won't catch on fire when he runs.

Human Speed

Runner Usain Bolt is the fastest human on Earth. In 2009, Bolt was clocked at 27.8 miles (44.72 km) per hour in a race. For nonathletes, a typical top speed is closer to 15 miles (24 km) per hour.

Fast Animals

Earth's fastest land animal is the cheetah. It can run in bursts at 70 miles (112.6 km) per hour. In the sea, the sailfish is the fastest. This super swimmer can reach speeds of 68 miles (110 km) per hour.

WALKING ON WATER

In the first *Incredibles* film, Dash runs across water without sinking. Impossible? Nope! A person with superhuman speed could really do that—and some real-life critters do it all the time. Let's see the science that makes it happen.

Surface Tension

Water is made up of hydrogen and oxygen, which form water **molecules**. Water molecules are strongly attracted to each other. They are not as strongly attracted to air. This means that wherever water meets air, the molecules on the surface cling together extra tightly. This is called **surface tension**. In water droplets, surface tension pulls the water into a round shape, like a balloon.

Pond Skaters

Insects called pond skaters live on the surface of still ponds. Their bodies are designed to spread their weight over a large area. There is not enough weight at any one point to break the water's surface tension. The pond skaters walk on the water!

Running on Water

Lizards called basilisks can run on water for about 15 feet (4.6 m) before sinking. Birds called western grebes also run on water during takeoff. Both animals achieve this through a combination of speed, webbed feet, and surface tension.

SHAPE-SHIFTING

Baby Jack-Jack seems normal, with no super powers, until Syndrome tries to kidnap him. Then—WOW! Scared and mad, Jack-Jack shows that he is a shape-shifter. This means he can change his looks and shape at will. Can real creatures do that? You bet they can! Let's find out about some real-life shape-shifters and some cool shape-shifting technology.

Amoebas

An **amoeba** is a one-celled life-form. It can take many different shapes. It moves by sending out a shoot called a **pseudopod**. This word means "false foot." The pseudopod acts sort of like a tunnel. The rest of the amoeba's body flows through it to a new location. An amoeba can send out many shoots at the same time!

Octopuses

Octopuses have no skeletons. They're squishy all over, except for their beaks, which are superhard. Because of this, they can change their body shape to squeeze through tiny holes and cracks. Octopuses can also change their skin texture and color to match their surroundings.

Programmable Matter

Scientists are working to develop **programmable matter**. This is any substance that can be changed or controlled by people. For instance, a gel might turn hard when it gets shocked by electricity. Robots or even other materials could be programmed to form tools with different purposes, such as a single tool that changes in an instant from a wire cutter to a screwdriver to a knife. This technology will be super useful!

FIRE! FIRE!

When Jack-Jack is angry, he doesn't just change his shape. He also bursts into flame! Could real people ever do this? And if they did, what would happen? Let's take a look at the science of fire and how it relates to people.

Cool Flame

Flames are caused by **chemical reactions** that give off light and heat. Flames can be different temperatures. Wood fires and candles burn at about 2,000°F (1,093°C)—ouch! Other substances, such as some oils, waxes, and alcohols, burn at less than 300°F (149°C). Trained magicians and fire jugglers use flames like these in their acts—very carefully!

Sudden Fire

To **ignite** a fire, you usually need a match or a spark. But fires can start on their own if things get hot enough. This is called **spontaneous combustion**. It is most common in hay piles and **compost** heaps. It happens when **chemical** reactions create trapped heat. When the heat reaches a certain point, WHOOSH! Fire erupts!

Fire Suits

Firefighters wear fire-resistant suits to protect themselves from flames and heat. Fire suits have three layers. The outer layer is a tough fabric that won't rip. The middle layer is a moisture barrier that stops dangerous liquids from getting through. The bottom layer is fire- and heat-resistant.

WATER IN THE AIR

Let's chill out with Mr. Incredible's friend Frozone for a while! Frozone is able to pull water out of thin air and turn it into ice. Does air really hold invisible water? Yep, it sure does! Let's see how it works.

Water Vapor

Three of the most well-known phases of matter are *solid*, *liquid*, and *gas*. Water has each of these three phases. Water's gas phase is called vapor. **Water vapor** is invisible. Sometimes, though, water vapor forms tiny liquid drops that are too light to fall out of the air. These drops can collect into steam and clouds, which we can see.

Phases of Matter

In a gas, the particles in a substance are far apart and move around freely. Most gases float.

Gas

In a liquid, the particles are closer together, but they can still move around. Liquids flow.

Liquid

In a solid, the particles are squeezed tightly together and are fixed in place. Solids are hard.

Solid

As temperature rises, solids turn to liquids, and then liquids turn to gas. The specific temperatures needed to cause these changes are different for each substance.

Humidity

Humidity is a word that describes the amount of water vapor in the air. High humidity means the air contains a lot of water vapor. Low humidity means the air holds very little vapor. When Frozone tries to make ice during a house fire, he finds there is no vapor in the air. The hot fire burned all the humidity away!

Fog is a type of visible humidity.

Snowflakes

A snowflake starts high in the cold sky, when water vapor freezes around a dust or pollen particle. The icy particle falls downward. More water vapor freezes onto the particle as it falls, forming feathery arms. The weather conditions are always a little different, so no two snowflakes are alike!

FAST FREEZE!

Frozone works *fast*. He can instantly freeze water vapor into giant ice structures. In the real world, things can freeze just as quickly. Let's explore this cool topic!

Frozen Breath

YOU can do what Frozone does—on a much smaller scale! When you breathe out on a cold day, the water vapor in your breath freezes instantly. You see a cloud as the vapor turns into tiny ice crystals.

Quick-Freezing

A gas called **nitrogen** turns into liquid below −320°F (−195.79°C). Liquid nitrogen freezes living cells on contact. It is often used to quick-freeze foods. Doctors also use it to freeze moles and other blemishes off people's skin. They have to be quick so they freeze only the problem area and not the healthy skin!

Ice Geysers

Enceladus, one of Saturn's moons, is dotted with ice **geysers**! These geysers spew water vapor from deep beneath the moon's surface. The vapor freezes instantly when it leaves the ground. The frozen crystals blast into Enceladus's **atmosphere**, where they form an icy ring. Frozone would be impressed!

Illustration of geysers on Enceladus

PERSONAL IDENTIFICATION TECHNOLOGY

Edna Mode does top secret work, so she uses personal **identification** technology to protect her work space. Machines have to recognize Edna's palms, eyes, and voice before they will let her in. How does this technology work? Let's find out!

Palm Prints

Look closely at the palm of your hand. You will see lots of lines and wrinkles. Everyone has them, and the pattern is different in every person. Palm print identification scans these lines, along with tiny ridges on your skin. It compares the scanned image to a stored picture. If the images match, the ID is confirmed. Most new cell phones use fingerprint identification.

Eye Scanning

There are two types of eye scans. One type scans the blood vessels on the eye's back wall. This is called a retinal scan. The other type scans the patterns of the iris, which is the colorful ring of muscles around the eye's pupil. Which type of scan did Edna use? Who knows—maybe both!

Scan of the iris

Scan of the retina

Voice Recognition

Everyone has their own way of speaking. Your voice tone comes from your height, your weight, and the structural makeup of the vocal chords in your larynx, or voice box. Your speech patterns are your talking style—fast, slow, loud, soft, and so on. Voice recognition technology turns these things into spiky graphs. Every graph, or **voiceprint**, is unique. A computer uses voice prints to match spoken passwords to stored voice samples.

NO CAPES!

"No capes!" That's what Edna says in the first film when Mr. Incredible wants a cape on his new Supersuit. She knows that capes can be dangerous for Supers. A cape caused one Super to get pulled into a jet turbine, and another was sucked into a spinning **vortex**. Capes could cause other problems too. Let's see what they are.

Vortex

A vortex is a mass of spinning air or fluid. Vortices (the plural of vortex) have **suction** power, which means they pull things into their centers. They could definitely suck in a cape—and the person wearing the cape too! Real-world vortices include tornadoes and whirlpools. Tornadoes spin at speeds up to 300 miles (480 km) per hour!

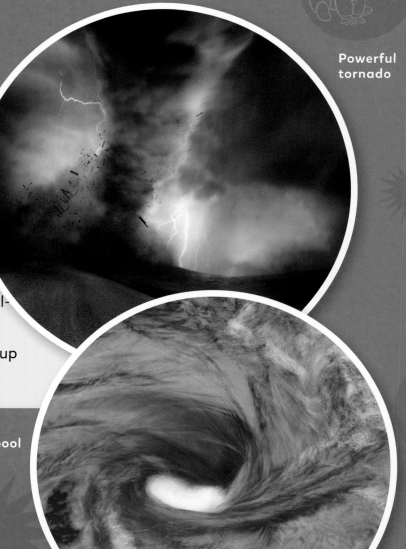

Powerful tornado

Whirlpool

Four Forces

Four forces work on a flying object. **Lift** pulls the object upward. Weight pulls it downward. **Thrust** pushes the object forward, and **drag** pulls it backward. Drag is created by air resistance. A cape would increase air resistance and slow the wearer down. That's bad news for busy Supers!

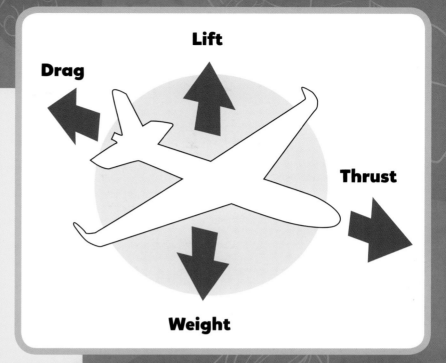

Lift

Drag

Thrust

Weight

Wings

Wings are sort of like capes for race cars. A wing, or airfoil, looks like a small, upside-down airplane wing. It is mounted across the back of a race car. The wing pushes the air up and forces the back end of the race car down. This is called **downforce**. Too much downforce can create drag. So racers always experiment with the angle of their wings. They try to find just the right balance between downforce and drag. A Super wearing a cape isn't able to change the angle of the cape. It just flops in the wind and causes a whole lot of drag for a soaring Super.

Wing on a race car

TRACKING DEVICES

Evelyn Deavor builds a tracking device for Elastigirl. This device tracks the Screenslaver's broadcast signal. Tracking devices are real, useful, and very common. In fact, you might be carrying one right now! *Are* you? Read on to find out and to learn more about this handy technology.

GPS

GPS stands for Global Positioning System. This system consists of a minimum of twenty-four Earth-orbiting **satellites**. At least four of the satellites are visible from any point on Earth at any moment. A GPS **receiver** on Earth measures the distance to all visible satellites. It uses this information to calculate its own position.

Phone Tracking

Smartphones contain GPS software. You can turn this software off, but most people don't. They leave it on all the time. Your phone constantly communicates with GPS satellites and tracks your position. Your phone knows where you are!

Turtle Power

Scientists use GPS technology to track many wild animals, including sea turtles. Receivers are glued to the turtles' shells. They collect location information wherever the turtles go. The information goes to a computer that maps the turtles' movements. This information helps scientists understand the turtles' habits and needs, which helps in conservation efforts.

Hawksbill sea turtle

Green turtle with satellite tag returning to the sea

ZERO-POINT ENERGY

"Zero-point energy. It's cool, huh?" Syndrome says in the first movie after he uses an energy ray to zap Mr. Incredible. The ray comes from Syndrome's gloves. These gloves collect power from tiny particles and turn it into a weapon. How does it work? Let's take a look!

What Is It?

Scientists believe there are many mysterious forms of energy in the universe. Zero-point energy is one of them. If this type of energy does exist, it would come from **subatomic** particles. This means particles that are smaller than **atoms**. These particles are never completely still. Also, scientists think they constantly flicker from one state to another. This activity might make energy that could be collected.

Illustration of an atom

First Use?

Some scientists think that in 2014 they used zero-point energy to create a pushing force. They say the push was very tiny, but it was there! No one else has been able to repeat these results, and many scientists don't believe it really happened. But who knows? If it did, it would be the first step into an exciting new field of science.

Zero-point energy field concept illustration

Master Blaster

An animal called the pistol shrimp has a built-in blaster! This little critter has one huge claw that it can snap with incredible force. It's kind of like a person snapping their fingers, but much harder. The snap makes a blast of sound and heat strong enough to stun other animals.

ROCKET POWER

In the first film, a boy named Buddy invents **rocket**-powered boots. Years later, when Buddy becomes Syndrome, he is still using them to fly around. He's also launching real rockets from his secret **bunker** on the island of Nomanisan. What is the science behind this technology? Let's learn about it!

Space shuttle *Atlantis* lifting off

Liftoff!

Rockets are full of fuel. When the fuel ignites, gases blast downward. This force pushes the rocket upward. A rocket must travel 25,000 miles (40,000 km) per hour to escape Earth's gravity and reach **orbit**. That's 7 miles (11.3 km) per second!

Hydroflyers

Hydroflyers work like rockets, but they use water instead of hot gases. A person straps their feet into the board's built-in boots. A hose delivers water to the device. This water blasts from nozzles on the bottom of the board with high force. The water jets push hard enough to lift the user 50 feet (15.2 m) into the air!

Space Walks

A **space walk** is when an astronaut leaves their vehicle to walk or float in space. Astronauts wear jet-powered backpacks during space walks. The backpacks have little nozzles that blast nitrogen gas. Astronauts control the blasts to push and steer them wherever they want.

MACHINES THAT LEARN

The Omnidroid featured in the first film can learn! By learning from its actions, it gets better and better at its tasks. Can real machines learn in this way? They sure can! Let's see what this ability is called and how it works.

Artificial Intelligence

Machines that learn are said to have **artificial intelligence**, or AI. This means that the machine can sense its environment and respond in ways that make the most sense at the moment. The reason it's called "artificial intelligence" is because these machines can seem smart—but they aren't. They are just collecting **data**. If an action fails, an AI machine records that. If an action succeeds, the machine records that too. Over time it learns the best way to do tasks.

Digital Helpers

Have you ever asked your phone to answer a question? If so, you have used a **digital** helper! These computer programs use voice recognition to understand your speech. Then they search the internet for answers. The more you use them, the better they "know" you. Their answers get more and more specific to your needs.

Deep Blue

Deep Blue was a chess-playing computer. It worked by looking at all possible moves and calculating their possible results. Deep Blue could **analyze** 200 million positions per second! In 1997 Deep Blue beat the world champion chess player, Garry Kasparov, in a six-game match.

INCREDIBLE ARMOR

The Omnidroid's surface is so hard that nothing can harm it except itself. Real-world **armor** isn't quite this tough. But it's true that some materials are harder than others—and all sorts of armor protect the wearer. Let's check it out!

Hardness

Natural substances called **minerals** are ranked on a **hardness** scale. The scale goes from one (softest) to ten (hardest). The softest mineral is talc, with a hardness of one. The toughest mineral is diamond, with a hardness of ten. No mineral can scratch a diamond except another diamond!

Diamond

Talc

Armored Clothing

Some **synthetic** fibers are used to make flexible armor for people. The molecules of these fibers are made in a lab, then spun into threads. The threads are woven into superstrong fabric. This fabric is used to make bulletproof vests and other protective gear. Superstrong synthetics include Kevlar, carbon fiber, and Lexan.

Natural Armor

Many animals have natural armor. The pangolin, for instance, is covered with hard, overlapping scales. Crocodiles are covered with bony knobs. Crabs and many other creatures wear their skeletons on the outside to protect the soft organs inside.

SEE YOU SUPER SOON!

With the help of the Incredibles and their friends (and even some enemies), you've learned a lot about super powers. You've learned a lot about science too. You can see that super powers may not exist, but the science behind them is very real indeed.

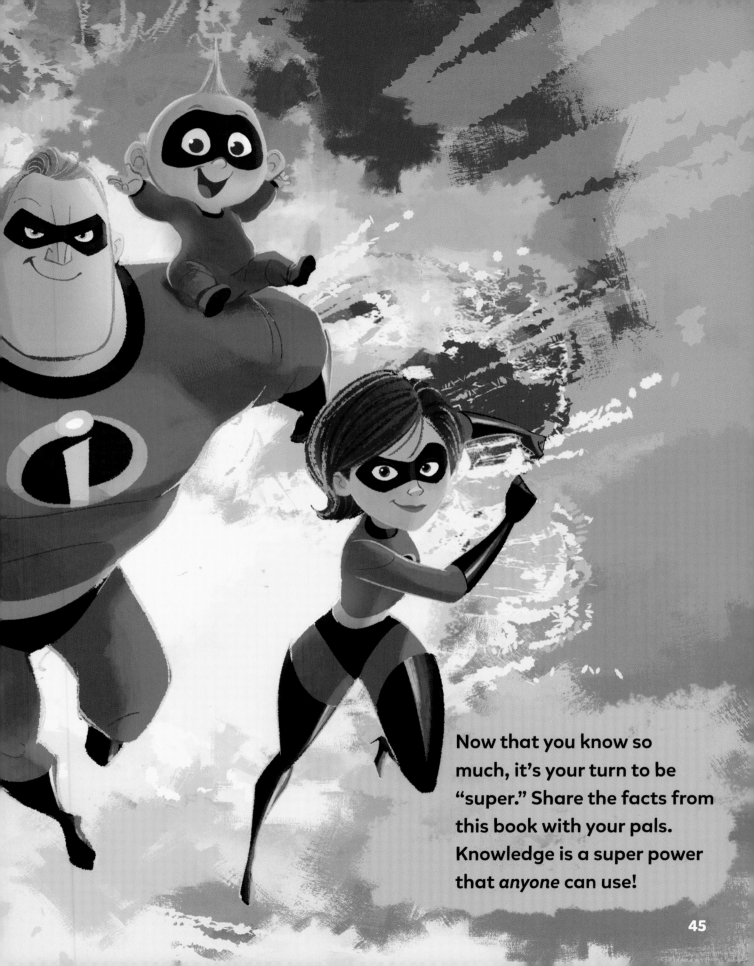

Now that you know so much, it's your turn to be "super." Share the facts from this book with your pals. Knowledge is a super power that *anyone* can use!

GLOSSARY

air resistance: the force that air exerts against a moving object. Air resistance slows objects down.

amoeba: a one-celled life-form that has no fixed shape. It can send out shoots in any direction in order to move.

analyze: to study or examine something carefully, in a step-by-step way

armor: any covering that protects a creature or object from harm

artificial intelligence: the ability of a machine to sense its environment and respond in a way that seems intelligent

atmosphere: a layer of gases that surrounds a planet or moon

atoms: the smallest units of matter and the basic units of chemical elements

attract: to pull or draw toward oneself by a physical force

barrier: something that blocks things from moving from one place to another

bunker: a reinforced shelter often used during wartime

camouflage: the ability to blend in with one's surroundings. Camouflage can include skin color, texture, and body shape.

cardiac: relating to the heart

cartilage: a hard but flexible tissue found in human and animal bodies. Unlike bone, cartilage bends easily.

chemical reactions: changes that happen when certain substances come into contact. A chemical reaction changes the original substances into new forms.

chemical: a substance created by or causing a change in another substance. All matter is made up of chemicals.

compost: rotting plant and animal matter

contortionists: people who can stretch and bend the body in extreme ways

data: pieces of information. Computers analyze data to reach conclusions or answers.

digital: describes any technology that uses number data to make calculations. Computers and anything computer-related are digital.

downforce: a downward force produced by airflow around the body of a moving object

drag: a force that resists a forward-moving object

electricity: a form of energy caused by the directional flow of charged particles

exercise: any activity requiring physical effort, done mainly to improve or maintain health and fitness

fibers: fine, threadlike pieces of material. Fibers can be woven together to form larger objects.

flexible: able to easily bend

force: anything that causes a change in an object's motion

force field: an invisible barrier that blocks objects or energy from passing through

friction: a force that is created when objects rub against each other. Friction creates heat.

geyser: a natural feature that blasts water, steam, or other substances out of the ground

gravity: a force that tries to pull two objects together. The more massive the object, the stronger the gravitational pull.

hardness: a measure of how much a substance resists being dented or scratched

hormone: a chemical produced by the body that makes organs or tissues do certain things

humidity: the amount of water vapor in the air. Humidity changes from time to time and place to place.

hydroflyer: a device that uses water jets to hover above a body of water

identification: the act of finding out who someone is or what something is

ignite: to start the process of burning; to set something on fire

invisible: not able to be seen by the human eye

lift: a force that pushes objects upward

magnetic: able to attract certain metals, such as iron. Magnetic objects, such as Earth, are surrounded by magnetic fields.

metamaterial: a material engineered to have unnatural properties

minerals: natural, nonliving substances with regular chemical makeups and internal structures throughout

molecules: groups of atoms bonded together to form stable substances

muscles: bands or bundles of tissue that pull to move body parts in people or animals

nitrogen: a common gas. Earth's atmosphere is about 78 percent nitrogen.

orbit: the path of an object going around another object in space

particles: very small bits of matter

programmable matter: a solid, liquid, or gas that can be controlled by a computer program

prostheses: artificial parts that replace parts of the body

prosthetics: the science of designing and creating artificial body parts

pseudopod: a shoot that extends outward from a cell. Pseudopod means "false foot."

radar: a system that uses energy waves to detect objects. Machines send out the waves. When they hit an object, they bounce back as echoes.

receiver: a device that collects incoming radio or electrical signals and converts them into a format that people can understand

repel: to push away using physical force

rocket: any device containing burnable material that makes a pushing force when ignited

satellite: an object that orbits another object. Satellites can be natural (like our moon) or manmade (like rockets).

skeletal: relating to the skeleton and bones

smooth: having a continuous, even surface

space walk: when an astronaut leaves a vehicle in outer space

spontaneous combustion: when something bursts into flame due to a chemical reaction

subatomic: smaller than an atom

suction: a force that pulls materials toward it. Suction works by reducing air pressure.

surface tension: the tendency of molecules to cling together at the surface of a body of water

synthetic: artificial or unnatural

technology: devices or techniques that solve problems or help people carry out everyday tasks

texture: the look or feel of an object's surface layer

thrust: a force that pushes objects forward or upward

voiceprint: a spiky graph that measures the qualities of a person's speech

vortex: a mass of whirling fluid or air that sucks things toward itself

water vapor: the gas form of water. Water vapor is invisible and is found throughout Earth's atmosphere.

wing: an aerodynamic device attached over the back of a car to cause a downward force and thus increase traction

wingsuits: one-piece jumpsuits with flaps of parachute fabric connecting the arms and legs. A person wearing a wingsuit can glide through the air.

zero-point energy: energy created by the constant movement of subatomic particles

INDEX

PHOTO CREDITS